1, 2, 3 Self-Care is Important to Me

A Colorful, Counting, and Rhyming Book

Written by : Dr. Jennifer Morgan

Illustrated by : Teena Rahim

Author's Note to Parents

Self-care is about making time to take care of your physical, emotional, and mental health. Parents can teach their children the value of self-care by helping them create healthy habits every day. Self-care habits do not need to be expensive or time-consuming, but they are most effective when practiced frequently and consistently.

Through vibrant illustrations and rhymes, 1, 2, 3 Self-Care Is Important To Me was written to empower kids with the understanding of what self-care looks like at a young age. This book is the first of a new collection of books that is meant to help parents, teachers, and therapists teach children how to help take care of their mental health.

For inquiries or more information, address: info@c4collection.com.
For more books and merchandise from C4 Collection, visit us at www.c4collection.com.
ISBN: 979-8-9854261-0-6

To C4, Atlas, Kj, and Kamdyn, always know you
are important, loved, and wonderfully made in
God's image.

To my husband, Clifton III, and my parents, Joe
and Vedia, without you, this book would not exist.
Thank you.

Hi friends! My name is KJ, and I am 7 years old.

Last spring, I experienced something strange. I stopped going to school, playing with friends, and my family's holiday plans changed.

I learned it was because of the covid-19 virus, and it was safer to social distance or stay in.

I also heard on the news that black and brown people were being treated unfairly because of the color of their skin.

A lot of things felt different last year, but I experienced good things too. My parents taught me how to cope with self-care and said that it was something I could do.

I asked my dad, "What does self-care mean?" He said that self-care is making sure I do things every day that make me feel happy, healthy, and sometimes even clean.

Hmm... that sounds easy to me!

Now that I know what self-care means, I will complete at least 10 activities every day as part of my routine.

First, I wake up and do **1** minute of deep breathing to start my day. My mom and I put our hands on our bellies and breathe slowly because that's the right way.

I first thought deep breathing was silly because I already know how to breathe, but deep breathing is different. It makes your body feel calm and more at ease.

For morning breakfast, I choose **2** healthy foods to eat, to help me stay alert in class while sitting in my seat.

The best thing about self-care is that you can do it anywhere. I'm now back in school, so I also do it there.

But before I leave for school, my mom and I think of 3 or more positive affirmations to say out loud. My favorites are, I am brave, I am smart, I am black, and I am proud!

I am
brave
I am
smart
I am black,
and
I am proud!

At school, I have **4** good thoughts that make me feel happy. If I worry or think too much about what I don't like about my day, I sometimes get a little snappy.

To keep my happiness, I find **5** more activities to do for fun, starting with running during recess and getting some sun!

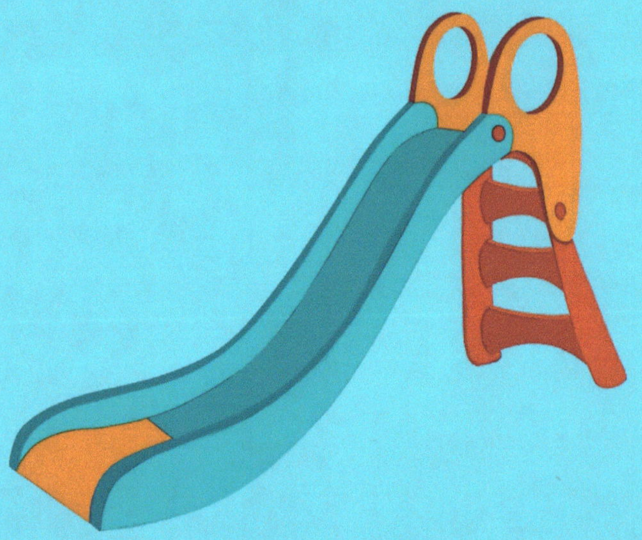

While at recess, I do **6** exercises to make me feel stronger. If I'm really enjoying it, I work out a little longer.

After school, I eat a snack and take a 7 minute mindful walk with my grandma and pet cat. Mindful walking is paying close attention to what surrounds me, including the things in nature that I hear, smell, feel, and see.

At dinner, I spend **8** minutes with my family talking about my favorite and least favorite parts of the day. When we're finished eating, my parents and I grab a board game for all three of us to play.

I have down time before bed in my room at night.

There are **9** muscles I stretch and a book I read before falling asleep with my favorite night light.

I get **10** hours of sleep with my favorite teddy bear. It makes me feel rested, restored, and ready for another day of self-care.

night